THIS BOOK IS DEDICATED TO THE TWO BROTHERS
FROM DIFFERENT MOTHERS WHO TAUGHT ME TO

# LOVE THE BIG EASY.

*Laissez le bon temps rouler*

ISBN: 978-1-7344666-7-6
Copyright September 2020
Follow The History Tree Series at
www.historytreeseries.com

f @oldtreesrock

𝕏 @history_tree

📷 @historytrees

I0145645

The Dueling Oak tree in the New Orleans City Park drips with Spanish moss.

To find it, when you see the stone bridge,
just walk across.

Reader Guidance: Built in 1902, this is the Pichot Stone Bridge. This rough-hewn cobblestone bridge was dedicated in the memory of Henrietta M. Leonie Pichot for her gift of $192.00 in 1901 to City Park. In today's park, you'll find it on your right when you walk down Dreyfous, just before Anseman Avenue. It has water under it only when Bayou Metarie is high enough.

At 300 years old, The Dueling Oak has seen a lot.
Have you ever wondered what a tree like that would say…
if it could talk?

Long before ivy climbed The Dueling Oak's bark,
bayou banks were perfect for canoes to embark.
Chitimacha people carved boats from cottonwood
Traveling and hunting the waterways was good.

READER GUIDANCE: The original inhabitants of the land that New Orleans sits on were the Chitimacha, with the Atakapa, Caddo, Choctaw, Houma, Natchez, and Tunica tribes inhabiting other areas throughout what is now Louisiana.

The tribes and our storyteller tree were there when two Canadian brothers explored future Jackson Square.

Reader Guidance-Pierre Le Moyne d'Iberville, a Canadian soldier and explorer, is often described as the founder of the first permanent French settlement in Louisiana. Iberville traveled on an expedition that arrived in Louisiana in 1699, after a prestigious and lengthy career with the military in New France. Iberville explored the lower Mississippi River Valley with his younger brother Jean-Baptiste Le Moyne, Sieur de Bienville. Together they established Fort Maurepas, near present-day Ocean Springs, Mississippi.

Our Dueling Tree knew them as "Pierre and Jean Baptiste."
School children recognize them as Iberville and Bienville.
They were pioneers, to say the least !

Reader Guidance- In the late sixteenth and early seventeenth centuries, Iberville made repeated trips between the lower Mississippi River Valley and France, ensuring the establishment of the new colony. Bienville assumed command of Fort Maurepas when the commandant of the post died in 1701. Upon Iberville's final return to Louisiana in 1702, Bienville was appointed governor of the colony and ordered to lead the construction of a post on Dauphin Island and another (Fort Louis) at Mobile. As Commandant, Bienville established a town on the east bank of the Mississippi where it made a "fine crescent" and named it after the Duc d'Orléans. In 1722, La Nouvelle-Orléans, or New Orleans, became the capital of the colony of Louisiane.

A "crescent" is a curvy shape, like the moon when it is skinny.
The brothers built where the Mississippi bends,
so New Orleans is the "CRESCENT CITY."

Iberville and Bienville arrived on a Tuesday,
a "FAT TUESDAY,"
and Mardi Gras had begun !
Dueling Oak saw the start of purple, green, and gold FUN !

Reader Guidance: Iberville and Bienville landed at the mouth of the Mississippi River, a place they nicknamed "Point du Mardi Gras" on the day that coincided with Fat Tuesday in France. This event was in 1699. Since then, even though historical accounts differ about the following several years, Mardi Gras has remained a beloved staple of New Orleans culture.

Dueling Oak lives in a city known for food, fun, and football.
But that food and fun was not always open to all.

In 1710, The Dueling Oak met people with dark skin
They were kidnapped from the villages they lived in.
Shipped from Africa to the Crescent City,
Families spent centuries as slaves, bought and sold without pity.

Reader Guidance: After the U.S. banned international slave trading in 1808, more than 1 million people were forcibly moved from the Upper South to the Lower South. Many of those individuals passed through New Orleans, which was the largest slave market in pre-Civil War America. Often the first stop was the slave markets of New Orleans where families were divided and sold away separately. New Orleans has very few physical markers commemorating its history as the receiving port for ships full of human cargo several times a month.

President Thomas Jefferson made the Louisiana Purchase in 1803. As young America grew, it included The Dueling Oak Tree.

LOUISIANA

Reader Guidance: Thomas Jefferson was the American president at the time of the Louisiana Purchase. The United States initially wanted to buy only New Orleans and the land around it. The purchase met with the strong opposition in the States on account of being unconstitutional. Those accusations were accurate, at least to some extent. President Jefferson couldn't deny that the Constitution of the United States did not provide for acquiring new territories but still he decided to proceed with the purchase since the removal of French presence in the region was such an important issue.

Our Dueling Oak once met a pirate- or should we say "privateer."
Jean LaFitte fought British Redcoats, before he took another career.
Some say he was a charming gentleman.
Some say he led a very bad clan.
You decide, whether war hero or robber,
Lafitte was a New Orleans Founding Father.

Reader Guidance: Few verifiable facts are known about Lafitte's life. But technically, Lafitte wasn't a pirate. He was a "privateer." It is an important distinction because piracy was illegal and punishable by death. What was the difference? A letter of marque from a nation at war labeled one a privateer with legal clearance to attack, capture, or plunder ships flying the flag of an enemy nation. With that letter of marque he allegedly helped Andrew Jackson save the city at the Battle of New Orleans. Despite the absence of facts, Lafitte is romanticized as a swaggering, swashbuckling man of mystery. A reflection of New Orleans herself, he was charming, roguish, and unapologetic of making his own rules.

The Dueling Oak was over 100 years old
when a man on horse arrived in the December cold.
Andrew Jackson was sick and cross,
but just the right man to be the army's boss.

READER GUIDANCE: On December 01, 1814, future President Andrew Jackson arrived in New Orleans to prepare for the inevitable attack on the city by the British during the War of 1812. He did not have much time to settle into his new post. The first engagement with the "Redcoats" took place on December 14 at Lake Borgne. The final Battle of New Orleans was fought on January 08, 1815, the last major battle of the War of 1812.

Our favorite pirate (ahem, privateer)
joined up with General Jackson.
At the Battle of New Orleans, Louisianans got in on the action.
With LaFitte's fighting ships, and the land battle on Jackson's shoulders,
The Dueling Oak saw Americans defeat the British soldiers!

Reader Guidance: The 1815 battle was between the British Empire and new territories in the United States of America. The British thought that capturing New Orleans would give them control of the vast majority of the newly acquired Louisiana Purchase. Waged on the grounds of the Chalmette Plantation, 5 miles southeast of the city, the conflict is thought to be the greatest American land victory of the war by many historians. It was an overwhelming victory for a raggedy group of draftees, pirates, gentlemen, and slaves. Led by Jackson, a sickly half-dead general with a short fuse, they fought off the greatest fighting machine in the world and won!

So why is our oak called The Dueling Tree?
'Cause there men would fight when they didn't agree.
They'd meet 'neath the branches with a sword or a gun
While folks gathered 'round to find out who won.

Reader Guidance: Here's a fun myth associated with the "Dueling Oaks." An 1892 Times-Democrat article noted that "Blood has been shed under the old cathedral aisles of nature. Between 1834 and 1844 scarcely a day passed without duels being fought at the Oaks. Why, it would not be strange if the very violets blossomed red of this soaked grass! The lover for his mistress, the gentleman for his honor, the courtier for his king; what loyalty has not cried out in pistol shot and scratch of steel! Sometimes two or three hundred people hurried from the city to witness these human baitings. On the occasion of one duel the spectators could stand no more, drew their swords, and there was a general melee."

Until the 1940's our Dueling Oak tree had a twin.
So what happened to the other?
A hurricane came and our tree lost its brother.

The Dueling Oak twins were separated by the "Hurricane of 1947." Forty-nine of the 273 hurricanes making landfall from the American Atlantic coast came across Louisiana between 1851 and 2004. The Hurricane of 1947 made landfall on Sept 19 with wind gusts of 112 mph claiming 51 human lives and flooding Jefferson Parish to a depth of over 3 feet. The levees along the shore of Lake Pontchartrain's south shore were built in response to this loss and destruction. The remaining oak is thought to be 300 years old with a height of 70 feet and a girth of 25 feet.

A hurricane is a very big storm, and part of almost everyone's Crescent City story. Super strong winds knock things down. Even huge old oaks breakdown or drown.

Our Oak friend endured a hurricane one dark September
that everyone in New Orleans will always remember.
Her name was Katrina, and when she darkened the sky,
our Crescent City tree saw thousands of people cry.

Reader Guidance: Early in the morning on August 29, 2005, Hurricane Katrina struck the U.S.
Gulf Coast  When the storm made landfall, it was a Category 3 rating with sustained winds of
100-140 miles per hour-and was a vast 400 miles across. The storm itself did a great deal of
damage, but its aftermath was catastrophic. Collapsed levees created to massive flooding.
Hundreds of thousands of people in Louisiana, Mississippi and Alabama fled their homes.
Hurricane Katrina caused over $100 billion in damages, killed nearly 2,000 people, and affected
90,000 square miles of the United States.

The Dueling Oak survived to tell us stories of voodoo and jazz.
New Orleans is unique, with things no one else has!
Our History Tree knows a bit about voodoo and Marie
Laveau. Don't be scared-we'll go slow...

Reader Guidance: Marie Laveau, the "Voodoo Queen of New Orleans" was a black priestess of astounding beauty, Madame Laveau wielded tremendous power in her community and rumors of her magical abilities were so persistent that visitors still visit her grave to leave tokens in exchange for small requests.

Voodoo is a religion from West Africa. It came in the ships with slaves. You'll find gris-gris dolls, and Voodoo Queens that *SHOULD* be in their graves.

Reader Guidance: New Orleans Voodoo is also known as Voodoo-Catholicism. It is a religion connected to nature, spirits and ancestors. Voodoo followers fleeing Haiti after the 1791 slave revolt moved to New Orleans. It gained popularity as many freed people of color made its practice part of their culture. Voodoo queens and kings were powerful political, as well as spiritual leaders in 1800s New Orleans. The core belief of New Orleans Voodoo is that God does not interfere in daily lives, but spirits can and do. Connection with these spirits can be obtained via musical, dance, chanting and snake rituals. Today you can find gris-gris dolls, potions and talismans in stores and homes throughout the city.

New Orleans is the birthplace of a special music called "JAZZ!"
If you add some brass to a piano and Caribbean drums,
jazz will blast you out of the doldrums!

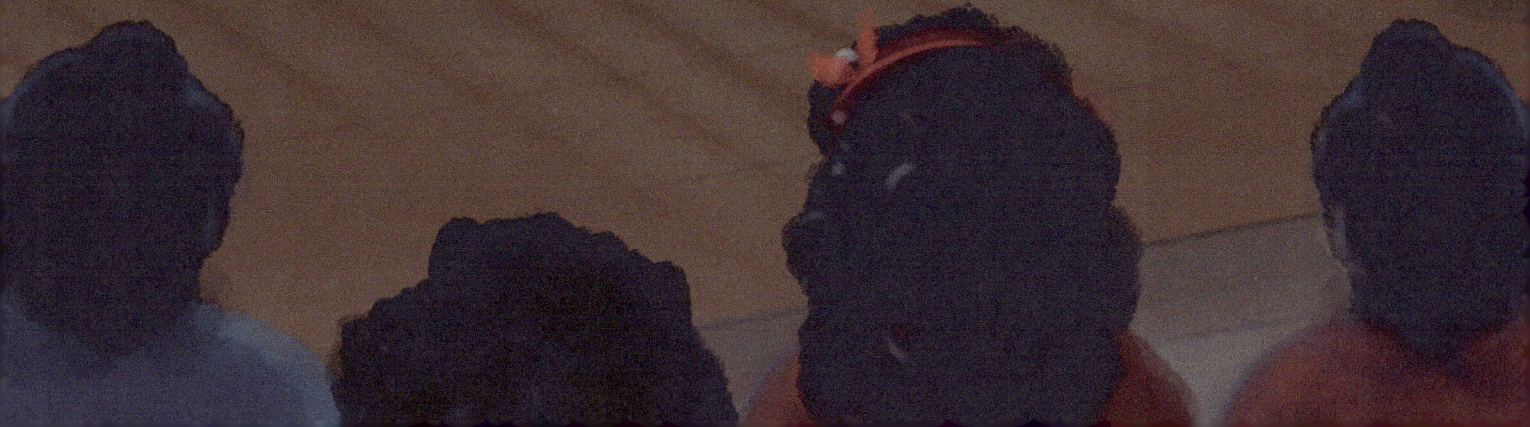

Jazz notes wafted through the branches in 1895.
A man named "Buddy" Bolden made his cornet come alive!
From Bolden to Marsalis, from "second lines" to Latin grooves,
jazz is bliss, and you'd be remiss, not showing off your moves!

Reader Guidance: New Orleans native Wynton Marsalis, according to his own biography page, "is an internationally acclaimed musician, composer and bandleader, an educator and a leading advocate of American culture."

"Second line" parades came from the city's famous jazz funerals. There are dozens throughout the year, usually on Sunday afternoons, in the French Quarter and neighborhoods all across the city. They include a brass band, jubilant dancing in the street and members decked out in a wardrobe of brightly colored suits, sashes, hats and bonnets, parasols and banners. They are a high energy moving block party!

If New Orleans jazz had an inventor, that person would be Charles "Buddy" Bolden. But although he is celebrated as a seminal figure in jazz at the turn of the 20th century, very little is actually known about the African-American cornetist and composer's life. There are no existing recordings of Bolden, who spent more than 20 years in an asylum before his death in 1931.

Food, food, food! Trees don't eat, but Dueling Oak knows it's GOOD!
Beignets at Café Du Monde? You know you should.
Gumbo every day? If only you could!
Whatever YOUR favorite, the menu in "The Big Easy"
puts everyone in a happy mood!

Reader Guidance- "The Big Easy" is a nickname for New Orleans referring
to the easy-going, laid back attitude toward life that residents enjoy there.

Another nickname for Dueling Oak's town is "The Paris of The South."
So the Lily Flower, or fleur-de-lis, is a city symbol without a doubt.

Reader Guidance: New Orleans has adopted the fleur-de-lis as a symbol of cultural identity and pride. The fleur-de-lis (sometimes spelled fleur-de-lys) has connections from ancient Egypt and Babylonia, to the Roman Catholic church and the French monarchy. Representations span from a symbol of purification and luxury to one of slavery and punishment. One legend identifies it as the lily given at his baptism to Clovis, king of the Franks (466-511), by the Virgin Mary. The lily was said to have sprung from the tears shed by Eve as she left Eden. The "symbol of purity" is also associated with the sanctity of Mary by the Roman Catholic church.

A Fleur de Lis on a gold helmet can only mean
The New Orleans Saints !

In Dueling Oak's town, a "'Dome" win is every fan's plan,
So grab your jersey and face paint with that fleur de lis brand!

New Orleans is mossy and peeling and hot.
It's Monday red beans and rice in a hot pot.
She's something special, all the way down to her trees
. So protect old history trees like the Dueling Oak, please.

Because if old trees could talk,
their stories would ROCK!!

## ABOUT THE AUTHOR

Tana Holmes is an award-winning thirty-year professional public-school educator, a mom, and a nature lover. She lives in Texas with her Louisiana transplant husband and two rescue dogs. She loves any opportunity to take I10 east to The Big Easy for a muffuletta at Central Grocery and beignets at Café du Monde. Her History Tree Series characters are eyewitnesses to history-making events. All of these ancient trees still stand as engaging educators for children of all ages interested in learning and loving their heritage. As more volumes in the series debut, Tana anticipates an opportunity to reach children globally with their own local "celebritree" storyteller. Visit her and the History Trees at www.historytreeseries.com If you enjoyed The Dueling Oak, add ALAMO TREE, and The Old Patriarch Tree to your library. They are available wherever you buy books- and don't forget to leave a review!

## ABOUT THE ILLUSTRATOR

Mahfuja Selim is a freelance illustrator mostly working on Children books for 8 years. She loves creating characters and locations that come from around the world. Her semi-cartoony drawing style sets her apart in the field. Her work has been published throughout the world in children's books, magazines, educational publications, children's games and packaging. She works with modern digital drawing tools at hand combined with all the traditional knowledge. Children love her work!

www.ingramcontent.com/pod-product-compliance
Lightning Source LLC
Chambersburg PA
CBHW042355030426
42336CB00029B/3488

* 9 7 8 1 7 3 4 4 6 6 6 7 6 *